W9-CON-830

ENDANGERED!

WOLVES

Ruth Bjorklund

 **Marshall Cavendish**
Benchmark

New York

For Marc, Lily, and Neil

Marshall Cavendish Benchmark
99 White Plains Road
Tarrytown, New York 10591
www.marshallcavendish.us

All Web sites were available and accurate when this book was sent to press.

Editor: Karen Ang
Publisher: Michelle Bisson
Art Director: Anahid Hamparian
Series Design by: Elynn Cohen
Cover Design by Kay Petronio

Library of Congress Cataloging-in-Publication Data

Bjorklund, Ruth.
Wolves / by Ruth Bjorklund.
p. cm. -- (Endangered!)
Includes bibliographical references and index.
Summary: "Describes the characteristics, behavior, and plight of
endangered wolf species, and what people can do to help"--Provided by
publisher.
ISBN 978-0-7614-2993-7
1. Wolves--Juvenile literature. I. Title.
QL737.C22B54 2009
599.773--dc22
2008022990

Front cover: A gray wolf
Back cover: An Arctic wolf (top); A gray wolf pup (bottom)
Title page: A gray wolf pup howling

Photo research by Pamela Mitsakos
Front cover: Mary McDonald/ Minden Pictures
The photographs in this book are used by permission and through the courtesy of:
Minden Pictures: Larent Geslin, 34, 37, 39; Tui de Roy, 40, 42, 44; Pete Oxford, 41. Alamy: Michael DeYoung, 1; Juniors
Bildarchiv, back cover (bottom); Kent Foster, 8;Yva Momatiuk & John Eastcott, 12; Carol Lee, 14; Mike Lane, 15; tbkme-
dia.de, 17; blikcwinkel/Meyers, 19; D.Robert Franz, 21; Malcolm Schuyl, 25; M. Timothy O'Keefe, 28; Stone Nature
Photography, 31; Andrew Harrington, 35, 38. Corbis: John Conrad, 4; Images.com, 6; William Campbell/Sygma, 10, 24;
Martin Harvey, 32; Frans Lanting, 43.Photo Researchers, Inc.: Thomas & Pat Leeson, 26. Nature Picture Library: Staffan
Widstrand 9. Shutterstock: Denis Pepin, back cover (top).

Printed in China
1 2 3 4 5 6

Contents

1

An Introduction to Wolves

Hundreds of thousands of wild wolves once ranged across many continents—Europe, Asia, Africa, and North America. Wolves are the largest members of the dog family. There are two **species,** or types, of true wolves in the world, the red and the gray. There are many subspecies of the gray wolf and there are two other members of the wolf family that are very closely related to true wolves—the Ethiopian wolf and the maned wolf. All

A gray wolf peeks from behind a tree. Most wolves avoid coming into contact with humans.

wolves have strong muscular legs, keen senses of smell and hearing, and very good eyesight. Wolves can smell a scent more than 1 mile (1.6 kilometers) away and can hear sounds nearly 6 miles (9.6 km) away. They are carnivores, or meat-eaters, and hunt other animals for food. Wolves stay hidden from view as much as they can and call to each other with yips, barks, and eerie, wailing howls.

In myths, stories, and legends, wolves have been portrayed as smart killers out to harm humans.

Since ancient times, many people around the world have lived in fear of the wolf or regarded it as a devil, a thief, or an outlaw. In myths and legends, the wolf was usually the evil one, such as in the tale of "The Three Little Pigs" or "Little Red Riding Hood." More than a thousand years ago, people believed that evil men lurking in dark corners were werewolves—creatures that were half human and half wolf. But some people in other cultures worshipped the wolf. The Mongols in Central Asia believed that their first ancestor was the wolf. Egyptians believed that the wolf was the god of the dead. Mars, the Roman god of war, was symbolized by a wolf. In the book the *Jungle Book*, kindly wolves raised the orphan boy Mowgli. In North America, Native Americans honored the wolf as a mighty spirit and great hunter.

Though wolves have rarely attacked humans, humans fear them and most do not want them living nearby. For centuries, humans and wolves shared the same **habitats,** and were in competition with one another for territory and food. Humans hunted the same **prey** as wolves, such as deer, moose, elk, buffalo, beaver and rabbit. Most wolves are shy and avoid humans. But as human population has increased, wolves have been pushed farther from their native territories.

Deforestation and other forms of habitat destruction have taken away the natural homes of many animals, including wolves.

For the past two to three centuries, humans have cut down forests, burned grasslands, and destroyed the wilderness areas where the wolves live. Humans have established farms and cities and fenced off areas to raise livestock for food. As the wolves' habitats have disappeared, many face starvation. To survive, wolves have raided human settlements and killed domestic cattle and sheep. This outrages farmers and ranchers. To battle back, they set out traps and poison to kill wolves.

Governments have offered **bounties,** or money rewards, to hunters who would kill a wolf and bring back its hide.

Today, the number of wolves living in the wild has shrunk. In many parts of the world, they have nearly disappeared. Less than fifty wolves remain in the highlands of Egypt. In Europe, there are only a few **packs** of wolves in remote areas of Spain, Italy, and the forests

A wolf eyes a flock of sheep. With their natural habitats shrinking and their normal prey disappearing, wolves may hunt livestock for food.

of Finland. In Sweden and Norway there are fewer than 100 wolves. In England, there are none. Though there are many more wolves living in Russia, they are still hunted and bounties are still being rewarded for killing wolves. Wolves are also hunted and poisoned in China and India, and their habitats are being destroyed by rapid human development.

Many scientists and conservationists (people who work toward protecting wildlife) hope to learn more about wolves. This information will help them protect wild wolf populations.

In North America, wild wolves in Mexico have disappeared. Very few wild packs of wolves live in the lower forty-eight states of the United States, though thousands of wolves do continue to thrive in the wilderness areas of Alaska and Canada. In some countries, governments have passed laws to protect the wild wolves.

In the United States, wolves in the lower forty-eight states are protected under a law called the Endangered Species Act. This law protects plants and animals that are in danger of becoming **extinct.** Extinction is when the last remaining individual plant or animal of a species has died. Under this law, there are two categories— threatened and endangered. An endangered species is a species with a population that is shrinking rapidly, along with the habitat that supports it. When a species has not been seen in the wild for fifty years, it is declared extinct. A threatened species is at risk of becoming an endangered species.

2

Gray Wolves

Gray wolves are the largest members belonging to the wild dog family. Gray wolves are not all gray. They range in color from black, gray, brown, tan, to white. Most have a black tip on their straight, bushy tails. Gray wolves stand 26 to 32 inches (66 to 81 centimeters) high and are 5 to 7 feet (1.5 to 2.1 meters) long. Males are larger than females, weighing 50 to 150 pounds (22.7 to 68 kilograms). Gray wolves have big heads, yellowish eyes, and very large teeth. Their shoulders and back legs are

The fur of a gray wolf can be brown, gray, black, white, or a mixture of these colors.

narrow to help them run great distances on their long, powerful legs.

There are more than thirty subspecies, or types, of gray wolves around the world. In North America, there are five subspecies. These creatures range from the mountains and deserts of Mexico and the American southwest to the frozen northern **tundras** of Canada and Alaska. The smallest gray wolf lives in tiny remote

Some wolves, such as this Mexican wolf—or lobo—resemble domestic dogs. All wolves, however, are wild animals and should never be kept as pets.

pockets of Mexico, Texas, Colorado, Utah, Arizona, and New Mexico. It is known as the Mexican wolf or *lobo,* which is Spanish for wolf. It is extremely rare, and many believe the *lobo* is close to extinct in Mexico.

The other four subspecies live in the prairies, forests, grasslands, mountain and tundra wilderness areas of the United States and Canada. With about 50,000 wolves, Canada has more wolves living in the wild than any other country but Russia. Most of the gray wolves found in the United States live in Alaska. In Canada and Alaska there are gray wolves that are completely white, known by the common names Tundra wolf or Arctic wolf. These wolves are larger than other gray wolves. Most of the wild gray wolf packs in

An Arctic wolf's white fur helps it blend in with the snow and ice.

the lower forty-eight United States live in Michigan, Idaho, Minnesota, Montana, Wyoming, and Washington state. They are sometimes called timber wolves.

SOCIAL LIVES

Gray wolves are very social animals. They live in closely knit family groups called packs. Each wolf has a certain place in the social order. Pack size ranges from two to thirty animals, though six to ten is most common. Each pack has a leader, called an **alpha** wolf. An alpha wolf has proven that he is the strongest and most successful hunter. He mates with the strongest female wolf. She is also called an alpha wolf. The alpha pair chooses the borders of the pack's hunting territory, which can be as large as 120 square miles (310 square km). Alphas lead the hunts, eat before everyone else, and decide where to stop and sleep at night.

Usually there is just one litter of baby wolves born per pack each year. Only the alpha female and the alpha male mate. Before the baby wolves, called pups, are born, the mother wolf builds a hidden den. She digs out a long tunnel, which opens up into a small area where the pups spend their first weeks. She keeps it spotlessly clean. Baby wolf pups are born blind and deaf. Their eyes are usually blue. In the first several weeks, the mother wolf does not leave her pups. The baby pups drink milk from their mother. Meanwhile, other members of the pack hunt for food to feed the mother wolf.

Some female wolves will dig tunnels or burrows for their pups. Others will use caves or other natural shelters.

When the pups are older, the mother wolf begins feeding them pre-chewed meat. After six to eight weeks, she leads them out of the den so that the pups can begin socializing with other members of the pack. Like any pup, baby wolves love to play. They chase each other around and pretend to fight. The adult wolves in the pack join them. Though they are only playing, the activities help the pups learn how to hunt and how to fit in with the social order. Teenage wolves are called cubs. Before they are old enough to join the adults to hunt for food the cubs stay behind, protected by the lowest member of the pack, the **omega** wolf.

A pack is usually made up of a pair of alpha wolves, their children, and some of their brothers and sisters. If there is plenty of food in their territory, a wolf pack may grow too large. When this happens, the pack may break up and wolves will go out and search for mates to start their own pack. A wolf that leaves the pack is called a lone wolf. Lone wolves rarely survive very long if they do not find a mate and start a new pack. Wolves need each other to hunt successfully as a team and to give each other protection from other wolves. Usually, wolf packs respect each other's territory. When a new pack forms, it will not hunt in any other pack's territory.

COMMUNICATION

Wolves communicate in many different ways. They "speak" to each other during social visits and while they are hunting. When lower wolves approach the

Howling is one of the most common forms of communication among wolves. Body language also plays a part in how wolves communicate.

alpha they whimper and lay back their ears to show friendliness and respect. Mothers squeak lovingly at their cubs. When wolves are struggling within the pack to improve their social standing, they growl at each other and point up their ears and bare their teeth. Wolves bark when they are excited, when they are hunting, or if another animal is in their territory.

Gray wolves howl for many reasons. They howl when they are excited after a kill or when pups are born. They howl over long distances to call each other for help, to warn of intruders, or to ask to be joined in a hunt. Wolves howl before hunting or when looking for a mate. Their howls also show sadness, such as after the death of the alpha wolf. Each wolf has its own howl. When gray wolves howl together, it makes an amazing chorus.

HUNTING

Gray wolves hunt in a pack, usually walking in a single line, following the alpha wolves. They can lope along for very

A wolf pack running at top speed can take down a larger animal, such as a moose or a deer.

long distances, gaining as much as 60 miles (96.5 km) a day. They can also run very fast for shorter distances. Gray wolves hunt in their own territory and regularly travel the boundaries. They mark the borders of their hunting grounds by going to the bathroom.

As the wolves travel, they look out for prey, though sometimes they just come across it accidentally. Wolves like to hunt larger animals, but prefer to attack only those that are sick, old, or weak. Once they spot their prey, wolves quietly surround it and then suddenly rush in for the kill. Often the prey is frightened and escapes the attack. Then the chase is on. Some wolves go after the prey while others wait to surprise it. If the animal tires, they all close in. After the pack has killed its prey the alpha eats, followed by the rest of the pack. Though wolves can eat a very large amount all at once, if there is food left over they will bury it for later. They will also carry meat back to the alpha female and her pups.

Depending on its habitat, a gray wolf will hunt and eat a variety of meat. In the north, Arctic wolves chase down large animals, such as moose, caribou, reindeer, and elk. When these animals are scarce, they will hunt and eat smaller creatures such as squirrels and rabbits. In the northern forests, wolves hunt for deer, elk, and moose. In the mountains and deserts of the western United States and Canada, wolves hunt bison, big horn sheep, mountain goat, musk ox, and antelope.

The gray wolf was once a very important part of the ecosystem. Gray wolves hunt prey that is weak in some way. They kill weak animals to leave more food for the strong ones. They also prevent overpopulation of animal herds. For example, when there are too many deer in a herd, the deer will over-eat tree bark and leaves and destroy their own source of food. Smaller creatures will eat the scraps left after a hunt. Raptors, such as eagles and vultures, eat the remains left by a wolf kill, along with other small animals such as crows, jays, foxes, hares, weasels, porcupines, and mice. Gray wolves are a healthy part of the ecosystem. But humans have killed off most of the wild wolf population and taken over the wolves' habitats, disturbing the balance of nature.

AT RISK

By the middle of the twentieth century, nearly all wolves in the lower forty-eight United States had been killed off. Some small packs remained in northern Minnesota and Michigan and a few Mexican wolves could be found in the southwest. After the Endangered Species Act was passed in 1973, gray wolves were listed as endangered in most of

This gray wolf is wearing a radio collar. Scientists use this to track the wolf's—and its pack's—movements.

the lower forty-eight states. Laws protected the wolves from ranchers and hunters. As a result, wolf packs from Canada could naturally migrate to northern states such as Montana, Washington, or Minnesota.

The U.S. Fish and Wildlife Service developed programs to help rebuild wolf populations. They captured wolves in Canada and placed them in the Rocky Mountains of Idaho and Yellowstone National Park— remote habitats where gray wolves had once thrived. Farmers and ranchers living nearby did not like the plan. But the government gave them permission to shoot wolves that attacked their livestock. By 2007, there were enough Eastern Timber wolves in Michigan and Minnesota that they could be taken off the list of threatened species. Packs of wolves in the Rocky Mountains and Yellowstone are growing.

Many hope that conservation efforts will help increase wild lobo populations.

The Mexican gray wolf has had a harder time recovering. Most experts believe that by 1980, all the wild Mexican wolves were gone. The United States and Mexico joined together to help the *lobo* recover. They captured a few wild Mexican wolves, which were **bred in captivity.** In 1998, they released thirteen wolves into a very remote and protected area in Arizona. In 2000, the first Mexican gray wolf pup from this program was born in the wild. Scientists hope to see one hundred Mexican wolves living in the wild in the near future.

3

Red Wolves

In the past, red wolves could be found from Texas across the southeastern United States to the Atlantic Ocean, and from Pennsylvania to the Gulf of Mexico. Red wolves are not red, but vary from brown to black with a reddish coloring to their fur. They are smaller than gray wolves, and are a little more than 2 feet (61 cm) high and about 4.5 to 5 feet (1.3 to 1.5 m) long. They weigh 40 to 80

Wild red wolves used to be numerous across much of North America. Today, however, their numbers are small.

With their narrow snouts and pointed ears, red wolves sometimes resemble coyotes or foxes.

pounds (18 to 36 kg). Red wolves have narrow faces with large, pointed ears and thin coats of fur. They have long legs and large feet and look somewhat like a German shepherd dog. When they are young, red wolves also look like coyotes.

Red wolves live in packs, but their packs are smaller, and usually have five to eight members. A pack is made up of an alpha male and female who mate for life, their offspring (pups), and sometimes the grandparents. Just one litter per year is born to a pack. Most red wolves leave the pack when they are one to three years old, and look for a mate to start a new pack of their own. Sometimes when an alpha pair has grown old, the pair gives up its leadership and lives with its offspring to help raise the pups.

In forests, marshlands, and coastal grasslands, red wolves hunt small game, such as rabbits, rodents, nutria, and raccoons. They do not always hunt as a group, but sometimes they will hunt as a pack to kill a deer. A red wolf eats only 2 to 3 pounds (0.9 to 1.3 kg) of meat a day. This is unlike a gray wolf, which can eat up to 30 pounds (13.6 kg). Depending on how many animals live in the area, the size of a red wolf pack's territory varies from 30 to 100 square miles (78 to 259 square km).

AT RISK

American farmers have clashed with red wolves for more than 250 years. Humans took over the red wolf's habitat for farmland and openly hunted red wolves to protect their livestock. As a result, red wolves ran out of food and places to live. They had become an endangered species. There were so few red wolves left that many of them mated with coyotes. By 1980, there were no pure red wolves living in the wild. Fortunately, biologists had captured some wild red wolves before they became extinct. They bred them in zoos and other safe places.

With time running out for the red wolf, the U.S. Forest Service developed a plan called the Red Wolf Recovery Program. In two wildlife refuges located on islands free from **predators,** the Forest Service raised the families of the pure red wolves they had captured more than thirty years ago. These islands—Cape Romain National Wildlife Refuge in South Carolina and St. Vincent National Wildlife Refuge in Florida—allow the red wolves to hunt, live in packs, and mate without bothering farmers.

Once the red wolf packs on the islands start to outgrow their territory, biologists set them free in a large wildlife refuge near the Alligator River in North Carolina.

Red wolves are very shy, so to track them, biologists place a radio collar on each wolf that they capture or release. The U.S. Forest Service hopes that through their program 220 red wolves will live naturally in the wild while more than 300 red wolves will live in wildlife refuges and zoos.

A red wolf is released after being caught, examined, and tagged with a radio collar.

4

Other Wolves of the World

Besides the gray wolves and red wolves, there are two other wolf species—the Ethiopian wolf and the maned wolf.

ETHIOPIAN WOLVES

Ethiopian wolves are the rarest wolf species and only live in eastern Africa, in the mountains of Ethiopia. These

Ethiopian wolves observe their territory from a rocky portion of the Bale Mountains.

wolves are also known as Abyssinian wolves or red jackals. They are smaller than gray wolves, weighing just 20 to 45 pounds (9 to 20 kg). They stand a bit more than 2 feet (61 cm) high, and are about 3 feet (0.9 m) long.

An Ethiopian wolf has a long, bushy tail and reddish-brown fur with white markings. The ears of the wolf are tall and pointy and its snout is long and narrow. For food,

An Ethiopian wolf sticks its narrow snout into a hole it has dug. The wolf is looking for mice and other small rodents that nest underground.

Ethiopian wolves hunt rodents such as rats, mice, gerbils, and moles. With their long snouts, they dig for prey in holes in the ground and under rocky outcroppings. Ethiopian wolves tend to hunt alone, because they do not need help with their small prey. Once in awhile, they do join together as a pack and hunt animals such as antelopes, lambs, and hares.

A pack of Ethiopian wolves relaxes in the afternoon sun.

Ethiopian wolves live in small packs. Three to thirteen animals may live in an Ethiopian wolf pack. Packs are led by an alpha male and an alpha female. Their young pups also live with them. When the pups are two years old, the females will leave the pack to begin their own families. As a result, a typical Ethiopian wolf pack is mostly made up of male wolves.

To protect her pups, the mother wolf builds a den with hidden tunnels beneath rocky cliffs. When the alpha wolf mother is home with the baby pups, the rest of the pack brings her food. Every wolf helps with necessary duties. Though they travel around alone, Ethiopian wolves meet during different times of the day to be sociable and to mark their territory's borders. All members of the pack help raise the pups and protect the family group from predators and enemy wolves.

There are fewer than 500 pure Ethiopian wolves in the world. Most of them live in a region called the Bale Mountains. Ethiopian wolves prefer high places with open, grassy areas. Though their territory is up as high as 10,000 feet (3 km), they still have problems with farmers and livestock. Farmers have been planting their crops higher up the slopes of mountains and are taking over more of the wolves' habitat. Farmers also keep dogs to protect their farms. The dogs compete with the wolves

Wolves that get too close to livestock can end up fighting with the ranchers' dogs or can get shot.

Wildlife biologists catch wild Ethiopian wolves so they can check on the wolves' health. Once they are done, they will release the wolves.

for food. The dogs sometimes even mate with the wolves, which further decreases the pure red wolf population. Since 2004, the Ethiopian wolf has been listed as an endangered species by the world-wide environmental group known as the International Union for Conservation

Ethiopian wolves tend to avoid interacting with humans, but human actions continue to endanger these animals.

of Nature and Natural Resources (IUCN). Scientists and concerned individuals dedicate a lot of their time to tracking and protecting these endangered wolves.

MANED WOLVES

Scientists and biologists do not completely agree whether or not the maned wolf of South America is a true

The grasslands in parts of South America are perfect hunting grounds for the maned wolf.

wolf. But using modern technology, most have come to accept that the maned wolf is the only wolf living below the equator. Many believe these wolves migrated south from North America. Today they are found in Brazil, Paraguay, Bolivia, and Argentina.

The maned wolf has reddish-yellow fur with black markings and a black mane. Its fur is thinner than other wolves, which helps to keep it cool in warm climates. The maned wolf weighs less than 50 pounds (22.6 kg) and stands 3 feet tall (0.9 m). It has long, thin legs that help it see above tall grass and long, pointy ears that swivel when the wolf is on the lookout for food or enemies.

Maned wolves do not live in large packs. Usually, a female wolf and a male wolf live side by side in neighboring hunting grounds. Though they mate for life, they do not spend much time together. Pups are born in early spring. Once the pups are two years old, they leave and set up their own hunting grounds and find their own mate.

Two maned wolves greet each other with careful body movements that show respect for one another.

The maned wolf is very shy. It lives in remote forests, **savannas**, and marshes and hunts at night. Hunting for food with their sharp claws, the maned wolf digs up lizards, mice, and snails. When hunting animals such as guinea pig, rabbits, and birds, the wolf leaps high and pounces on its prey. Unlike other wolves, the maned wolf also eats plants and fruits.

The IUCN has listed the maned wolf as a threatened species. Much of its habitat is lost when farmers burn

Using the muscles of its strong legs, a maned wolf pounces on its next meal.

As human settlements get closer to maned wolf habitats, encounters between people and wolves become more likely. In South America, some roads that cut through maned wolf territory have signs reminding drivers to be aware of nearby wolf populations.

grasslands and plant crops. Besides angry farmers who believe the maned wolf is killing their chickens, the wolf is also hunted by people who believe that wearing jewelry made of the wolf's body parts brings good luck. Conservationists continue their efforts to protect and increase wild maned wolf populations and educate more people about the danger these wolves are in.

Without efforts to protect wolves and their habitats, many wolf species may disappear forever.

Wolves play a very important role in the environment. They wander through the wilderness, hunting the sick and the weak, controlling other animal populations, and leaving more resources for strong, healthy animals. Their place in the food chain also helped small animals. No animal is their predator—except for humans. Humans have over-hunted these creatures, taken over their habitats, and destroyed much of the wolves' way of life. In many countries around the world, people are realizing that saving the wolves means saving many other wild animals and protecting the wilderness.

GLOSSARY

alpha—The first letter of the Greek alphabet used to describe the male and female leaders of a wolf pack.

bounty—A money reward, usually from the government, that is given to someone who captures or kills a predatory animal.

bred in captivity—The process for breeding rare animals in controlled settings, such as zoos or wildlife preserves.

extinct—No longer living.

habitat—The natural area where a plant or animal lives.

omega—The last letter of the Greek alphabet used to describe the lowest-ranking adult wolf in the pack.

pack—A family of wolves.

predator—An animal that hunts and kills other animals for food.

prey—Animals that are hunted as food.

savanna—A tropical grassland scattered with trees.

species—A type of plant or animal group that can reproduce together.

tundra—A cold, treeless plain with a lower level of soil that is permanently frozen. In summer, the upper layer of soil melts slightly allowing lichens, grass, small bushes, and moss to grow.

FIND OUT MORE

Books

Bailey, Jill. *Gray Wolf*. Chicago: Heinemann Library, 2005.

Barnes, Julia. *The Secret Lives of Wolves*. Milwaukee, WI: Gareth Stevens, 2007.

Kalman, Bobbie. *Endangered Wolves.* St. Catherines, Ontario: Crabtree Publishing, 2005.

Leach, Michael. *Wolf: Habitats, Life Cycles, Food Chains, Threats.* Austin, TX: Raintree Steck-Vaughn, 2003.

Web Sites

International Wolf Center
http://www.wolf.org

Smithsonian National Zoological Park—Maned Wolf
http://nationalzoo.si.edu/Animals/Amazonia/Facts/manedwolf
    facts.cfm

U.S. Fish and Wildlife Service, Mexican Wolf and Red Wolf pages
http://www.fws.gov/southwest/es/mexicanwolf
http://www.fws.gov/alligatorriver

Wolf Haven International
http://www.wolfhaven.org

World Wild Wolves-Defenders of Wildlife
http://www.kidsplanet.org/www

INDEX

Pages numbers in **boldface** are illustrations.

ABOUT THE AUTHOR

Ruth Bjorklund lives on Bainbridge Island, a ferry ride from Seattle, Washington. She and her family have always loved the outdoors, especially the beautiful wild places that North American wolves historically call home.